# KOBE
# BRYANT

# KOBE BRYANT

## Basketball Big Shot

Jeff Savage

*For Christian*
*Shoot for your dreams!*
*Jeff Savage*
*Keep reading :)*

LERNER
**SPORTS**
AN IMPRINT OF LERNER PUBLISHING GROUP

*This book is available in two editions:*
Library binding by LernerSports
Soft cover by First Avenue Editions
Imprints of Lerner Publishing Group
241 First Avenue North
Minneapolis, Minnesota U.S.A. 55401

Website address: www.lernerbooks.com


Library of Congress Cataloging-in-Publication Data

Savage, Jeff, 1961—
    Kobe Bryant : basketball big shot / Jeff Savage.
        p.    cm.
    Includes bibliographical references and index.
    Summary: Profiles Kobe Bryant, who went straight from high school to the pros, becoming the youngest person ever to play in the NBA.
    ISBN 0-8225-3680-3 (lib. bdg. : alk. paper)
    ISBN 0-8225-9860-4 (pbk. : alk. paper)
    1. Bryant, Kobe, 1978—Juvenile literature. 2. Basketball players—United States—Biography—Juvenile literature. 3. Los Angeles Lakers (Basketball team)—Juvenile literature.
[1. Bryant, Kobe, 1978— 2. Basketball players. 3. Afro-Americans—Biography.] I. Title.
GV884.B794.S28 2001
796.323'092—dc21                          00-009162

Manufactured in the United States of America
1 2 3 4 5 6 — JR — 06 05 04 03 02 01

# Contents

*Kobe is often compared to Michael "Air" Jordan.*

# The Air Apparent

Kobe Bryant could feel the cold stare. He gazed at the ceiling of Madison Square Garden. Then he looked over at Michael Jordan. Jordan was chomping on a piece of gum. His eyes were fixed hard on Kobe. Shivers crawled up Kobe's spine. Kobe leaned close to **backcourt** teammate Gary Payton. "I'm nervous," he whispered.

Nervous? Kobe had a very good reason to be scared. He was about to play in the 1998 National Basketball Association All-Star Game in New York City. Fans across the country had voted for him to start at guard for the Western Conference. He hadn't even started for his own team, the Los Angeles

Lakers, all year. His average of 19 points a game off the bench for the Lakers matched his age. Kobe was the first teenager ever to start in the All-Star Game. Most players his age were in college, but Kobe had gone directly from high school to the pros.

NBA executives called him the "Air Apparent" to the great Jordan. On one side of full-page newspaper advertisements for the All-Star Game was Jordan. Kobe was on the other. "Cool," Kobe said when he first saw the ad. "It was like they were making it out to be some big one-on-one showdown." Kobe didn't feel so cool at the game. This was Jordan's final season, and he didn't want some kid stealing his all-star show.

The Eastern Conference won the opening tip, and Jordan scored the game's first points. But on the East's next possession, Kobe intercepted a cross-court pass. He threw it ahead to Kevin Garnett and got it back for an **alley-oop** slam. Kobe's dunk brought the fans to their feet. The replay on the arena's electric scoreboard ignited another roar. But Jordan answered with a dunk of his own, and then he drilled two fallaway jump shots. "When he hit those two shots," Kobe said, "I was like, 'Cool, let's get it on.'"

*Kobe slams home a dunk during All-Star weekend.*

Kobe's confidence is one of the reasons he is a popular player. He plays with flair, energy, and joy. He is hip and handsome, with a coffee complexion, long eyelashes, and a big smile.

There were plenty of stars in New York for All-Star weekend, but Kobe was the main attraction. Reporters surrounded Kobe, and the cameras followed his every move. Even when the other players were interviewed, they were asked about Kobe. Karl Malone said, "He is just so exciting to watch." Mitch Richmond said, "The thing I like about him most is that he has his head on straight. And he listens."

Kobe is 6 feet, 7 inches tall, with wide shoulders and a narrow waist. His body is not the only thing that reminds people of Michael Jordan. His baritone voice and thoughtful comments even sound like Jordan. Kobe says, "There can be no next Michael Jordan. I just want to be Kobe Bryant."

Once the game started, Kobe's butterflies disappeared. The next time he had the ball, he went straight up and popped a 10-footer over Jordan. Later in the first quarter, he flew down the lane for a 360-degree **helicopter dunk.** No wonder the fans love to watch him play. Kobe has a hop to his feet and a rhythm to his dribble. He has mastered the game's fundamentals, too. He makes smart passes and plays sticky defense. But it's his acrobatics that fans want to see. As one player said, "his game has all the *oohs* and *aahs*."

The Eastern Conference was comfortably ahead in the second half when Kobe and Jordan started a game within the game. Jordan faked right and left to fool Kobe and then lofted a **finger-roll layup** that Shaquille O'Neal **goaltended.** Kobe answered by putting the ball between his legs and around his back as he glided past Jordan to hit a neat running hook. Next, Kobe got out on a fast break and faked a pass with his left hand before flipping the ball softly into the net. "I was just trying to fend him off as much as I could," said Jordan.

By this time, the other players were clearing one side of the court so Kobe and Jordan could go one-on-one. The game had become a showcase for the league's past (Jordan) and its future (Bryant). After Jordan nailed a jumper, Kobe blew past Jordan and Grant Hill on his way to the basket. As Kobe soared through the air, he found his path blocked by 7-foot Dikembe Mutombo. Kobe faked a shot with his left hand and, while still in midair, twisted his body and with his right hand flipped the ball over Mutombo into the basket. "Unbelievable," David Robinson said.

In just 22 minutes, Kobe already had 18 points and six rebounds. During a timeout midway through the third quarter, a few of Kobe's Western Conference teammates grumbled that they weren't getting enough shots of their own. Coach George Karl put Kobe on the bench for the rest of the game. Jordan continued playing and finished with 23 points. He was awarded the game's Most Valuable Player trophy as his team won 135–114.

Afterward, Jordan praised Kobe. "He came at me pretty early," said Jordan. "I would if I was him. He attacked. I liked his attitude." At his locker, Kobe was asked if this game symbolized a passing of the torch from the great Jordan to him. "No, not really," said Kobe. "I just looked at tonight as a learning experience. . . . I just want to be the best basketball player that I can be."

Jordan heard other stars mutter that Kobe played too prominent a role in the game for someone so young. Jordan remembered hearing the same thing when he burst onto the scene many years earlier. He knew such talk might be painful to Kobe.

As Jordan left Madison Square Garden, he spotted Kobe in the arena's corridor and walked over to him.

*Kobe won the All-Star slam-dunk contest as a rookie.*

He looked into Kobe's eyes and said, "It's important for you to stay aggressive. You just have to continue to be aggressive." Kobe nodded and thanked him. Jordan turned and walked off. Kobe stood a moment more. Then his smile grew wide as he followed Jordan out the door.

Staying aggressive is exactly what Kobe did when he helped lead the Los Angeles Lakers to the NBA Championship in 2000. After a serious ankle sprain in game two of the finals against the Indiana Pacers, Kobe came back in game four with an overtime performance that will go down in sports history. As he later said, "It was just realizing the time to attack."

Kobe had just put up back-to-back jumpers over the Pacers' star player, Reggie Miller. Then, he leapt high into the air to retrieve a teammate's missed shot. When he brought the ball behind him for a put-back, only 5.9 seconds were left in the game.

Former NBA star Isiah Thomas was blown away by Kobe's game-winning basket. "Considering the injury he had and the circumstances, it was big time. He did it with such ice. What we saw was his intelligence catch up to his talent."

Kobe continued to shine in game six, when he and Lakers captain Shaquille O'Neal beat the Pacers

116-111 for the championship title. After such a stunning victory at the age of 21, the "Air Apparent" had one thing to say: "I can't wait to do it again."

*Kobe, touching the NBA trophy, greets the crowd at the Los Angeles Lakers' victory parade.*

*Kobe's senior photo from Lower Merion High School.*

# A Broad
# Education

Kobe Bryant had a basketball in his hands, his father says, "before he could even walk." This is no surprise to anyone who knows the Bryant family.

Kobe's mother, Pam, did not play pro basketball, but Pam's brother, Chubby Cox, was a college basketball star who played briefly in the NBA. Kobe's father, Joe, played 16 years as a professional, eight in the NBA. Joe was known as "Jelly Bean" Bryant because a fan once gave him jelly beans. Joe Bryant was a 6-foot-10 forward who played with flair for the Philadelphia 76ers, the San Diego Clippers, and the Houston Rockets. After his NBA career ended, Joe played for eight more years in the pro leagues in Europe.

Kobe Bean Bryant was born August 23, 1978, in Philadelphia, Pennsylvania. He was Joe and Pam's third and last child, following two girls, Sharia and Shaya. Kobe is a type of Japanese steak. His parents saw it on a restaurant menu a few days before his birth. Bean is short for Jelly Bean.

By the time he was three, Kobe was watching his father play basketball on television. Kobe would put his little hoop next to the TV and squeeze his Nerf basketball. When his daddy made a basket, Kobe would make one, too. Three years later, Kobe and his family moved to Italy. The Bryants lived in a town called Riete. Then they moved to Pistoia. Next they lived in Mulhouse, France, before returning to America eight years later. The Bryants were one of the few American families in Riete. Kobe learned to speak Italian at school. At home, he practiced new words with his sisters at the kitchen table.

In most European countries, basketball is a popular sport, but most children prefer soccer. After school, Kobe would practice his dribbling and shooting on the school playground until other children showed up and started kicking a soccer ball around. "I had to give up the court," said Kobe. "It was either go home or be the goalkeeper."

*Pistoia is a beautiful city in northern Italy. Kobe and his family lived there while his father played in the Italian pro league.*

Kobe's grandparents mailed videotapes of NBA games to Italy. Kobe enjoyed Larry Bird's passing and Michael Jordan's acrobatics, but mostly he loved seeing the moves of Los Angeles Lakers great Earvin "Magic" Johnson. After each Lakers game, Kobe would run outside and try to copy to moves he saw. He even had a life-sized poster of Magic on his bedroom wall. "Magic," Kobe says. "That's who I wanted to play like."

By the time he was eight, Kobe went to his father's practices every day. Sometimes Kobe played one-on-one with the Italian players. They would be easy on him, pretending to fall down so he could dribble by. But within a couple of years, Kobe could hold his own. Sometimes he even won. Joe would stand on the sideline, laughing at his teammates.

Kobe even practiced with the team. He learned picks, cuts, and smart passes. The Italian players shouted to him: "Tira la bomba!" (shoot the three) and "Bellissimo tiro!" (beautiful shot). During halftime of Jelly Bean's games, Kobe would scamper onto the court and shoot baskets as the crowd cheered. Kobe's schoolboy classmates weren't impressed. They told Kobe he wouldn't be such a great player when he went back to the United States.

When Kobe was 13, his family returned to the United States. Kobe found that the English he had learned from textbooks was nearly useless. "These kids weren't speaking English," said Kobe. "They spoke in dialect, slang. I couldn't understand a word they were saying." They teased Kobe for not being able to talk like they did. Kobe used basketball to communicate with others. "It definitely helped me make new friends," he said.

Kobe joined a summer league near his home in Ardmore, Pennsylvania. On the questionnaire, he wrote "NBA" as his future occupation. A camp counselor warned Kobe that he had a one-in-a-million chance. "I'm going to be that one in a million," he told the counselor. "You see Magic, Michael? They made it. What's the difference about them?"

Kobe starred as an eighth grader at Bala Cynwyd Junior High School and soon gained a reputation in town. Lower Merion High School coach Gregg Downer heard about him and went to see him practice. "I watched him play for five minutes," says Downer, "and I said to my assistant coach, 'This kid's a pro. He's going to be a pro.'"

At Lower Merion High School, Kobe studied hard and maintained a solid B average. For fun, he wrote rhyming songs with his friends. His hip-hop name was Kobe One Kenobe the Eighth. His pal Anthony Bannister explained that the name came from *Star Wars* "and Kobe's a star." But Kobe focused mainly on his first love. "Basketball was it," he said.

As a ninth-grader, Kobe was 6 feet, 2 inches tall and as skinny as a piece of spaghetti. But the fundamentals that Kobe had learned playing with his dad allowed him to play any position. Before long, he was a youngster dunkster. By his sophomore year, college scouts were watching him. One recruiter said, "The thing the scouts like so much about him, besides his talent, is his mentality. He's a very confident, very centered young man."

One time, Kobe had the flu, but he played anyway because the game was an important one. During warmups, he wrapped a towel around his head and sat at the end of the bench, far from his teammates so they wouldn't get sick. During the game, he played hard and helped build a large lead for his team, the Aces. Then he'd return to the bench and wrap his head with the towel. Another time, he broke his nose when he collided with an opponent. One of his eyes swelled shut. But Kobe insisted on staying in the game, and he led his team to victory.

Kobe's best practice came against his father. "I didn't beat him one-on-one until I was 16," Kobe said. "He was real physical with me. When I was 14 or 15, he started cheating. He'd elbow me in the mouth, rip my lip open. Then my mother would walk out on the court, and the elbows would stop. He didn't do it to hurt me, he did it to make me tougher."

Jelly Bean wasn't Kobe's only tough opponent. Kobe met Eddie Jones at **pickup games** at Temple

University's McGonigle Hall, and the two became good friends. Jones was a star for Temple. Kobe played often against Jones's college teammates, and Jones attended Kobe's high school games. Jones saw Kobe go the length of the court in four seconds to hit a shot at the buzzer to beat Coatesville High. He saw Kobe bury rival Ridley High by hitting 10 of 11 shots for 24 points—in the first half! In the play-offs, the Aces trailed Norristown by 10 points when Kobe drilled 9 of 10 second-half shots to win it. "I love to pass the ball," Kobe said, "but when it comes down to crunch time, I click it on. There's no doubt I want the ball."

At the suggestion of Kobe's father, Philadelphia 76ers coach John Lucas began inviting Kobe to practice with the Sixers. Kobe was just 16, but he noticed that he had little trouble keeping up with the pros. "Kobe was so dominant in there," said Fred Carter, another former 76ers coach, "that some days they had to get him out of the gym. He was demoralizing guys." Kobe remembers beating flashy Sixers star Jerry Stackhouse one-on-one. "I think I took him by surprise," said Kobe.

By Kobe's senior year, he had grown to 6 feet, 5 inches. He led Lower Merion High School to a 31−3 record and the Pennsylvania state title. He averaged 31 points, 12 rebounds, seven assists, four blocks, and four steals. He finished his career as the all-time leading scorer in southeastern Pennsylvania history with 2,883 points, breaking the mark of NBA Hall of Famer Wilt Chamberlain. Kobe was an easy choice as National High School Player of the Year.

Kobe's grades were good, and he scored an impressive 1080 on the Scholastic Aptitude Test. College recruiters begged him to play for their school. Kobe narrowed his choices to the University of North Carolina, the University of Michigan, the University of Kentucky, and Duke University. But plenty of NBA scouts were also in the stands at Kobe's games, too. Why? Kobe might skip college.

Most NBA players are former college players. Once they have finished playing college basketball, they are eligible for the NBA draft. Every summer, all the NBA teams gather to take turns choosing new players in the draft. Each team chooses two players, but often only one makes the team.

Only six players in the last 30 years had made an NBA team right out of high school. All six were forwards or centers. No guard had ever done it. "I don't know," said Kobe, "if I'm ready yet for the pros."

*Earvin "Magic" Johnson was Kobe's favorite Laker star.*

*Kobe's sister Sharia is one of his best friends.*

# A Kid in a Man's Game

On Monday, April 29, 1996, the final bell of the day rang at 2:25 P.M. as it did every school day. But most of the students at Lower Merion High did not head home. Instead, they hurried to the gymnasium to hear the big announcement. Kobe had called a press conference. Reporters from around the country encircled the basketball court.

Kobe looked fine in his coat and dress pants, with wraparound sunglasses resting on his shaved head. He waved to his family and stepped to the microphone. He smiled and said, "Hi, I'm Kobe Bryant, and I've decided to take my talent to, uh..." He paused and scratched his chin. "Well," he continued, "I have decided to skip college and take my talent to the NBA." The students erupted with a cheer as the reporters busily scribbled in their notebooks.

"I say why not? The opportunity is there," Kobe said. "I want to get out there and compete with the greatest players on earth now. I know Michael [Jordan] isn't going to be in the league forever, [Charles] Barkley, [Hakeem] Olajuwon. I want to get my crack at playing against those guys before they are gone." Kobe's announcement sparked a debate. Some praised him for his courage. Others, like NBA scouting director Marty Blake, were skeptical. "This kid," said Blake, "is making a catastrophic mistake."

Kobe finished high school with a flourish. His date to the senior prom was teenage singer Brandy. They had met a year earlier at a music awards show. At the dance, Kobe kept thinking to himself, "Wow, it's Brandy." But Brandy wasn't the only star at the prom. Kobe's classmates asked him for autographs, and he happily signed. Three weeks later, Kobe appeared on Rosie O'Donnell's TV show.

In the summer of 1996, Kobe traveled from city to city to attend predraft camps. Coaches and general managers check out prospective players for the draft at these camps. The Los Angeles Lakers general manager, Jerry West, wanted to see what Kobe could do. First, he asked Kobe to jump as high as he could toward the rim, and Kobe touched the top of the backboard square. Next, West tossed Kobe a ball and told him to try to score on former Lakers defensive wizard Michael Cooper, who was known for frustrating Larry Bird and Michael Jordan. Cooper could not defend Kobe.

*Kobe took singing star Brandy to his senior prom.*

West asked a couple of other players to guard the teenager. After Kobe blew past them, too, West whispered to an assistant, "I've seen enough. Let's go."

Kobe had been a Lakers fan since the days of Magic Johnson. What's more, Eddie Jones, his friend from Temple University, played for the team. But Kobe thought Los Angeles was picking too late in the draft to get him, so he put the idea of being a Laker out of his mind.

On the day of the draft, Kobe sat proudly among the top college players at New Jersey's Continental Arena and listened nervously as the teams made their choices. Kobe's family sat next to him, his mother squeezing his hand as the teams announced their choices. "Wherever I go," Kobe said to them, "I want you to go with me."

Then Kobe was drafted. The Charlotte Hornets selected him with their first pick, the 13th overall. "I am happy to be a Hornet," Kobe told reporters. "This is a great challenge."

Kobe immediately began hearing rumors that the Lakers wanted to trade for him. For two weeks, nothing happened. Then one day a trade was announced. The Lakers sent their veteran center Vlade Divac to the Hornets for 17-year-old Kobe Bryant.

"This is a dream come true," Kobe said. "It's the moment I've been waiting for."

Kobe signed a three-year contract with the Lakers for $3.5 million. He became a sportswear spokesman for another $1 million a year. Kobe moved west to Southern California with his mother and father and sister Shaya. His oldest sister, Sharia, remained in Philadelphia for her senior year at Temple University, and then she joined the rest of the family. Kobe bought a big house in Pacific Palisades, a few miles up the coast from the Forum where the Lakers played. The home has six bedrooms, a swimming pool, and a whirlpool bath. Kobe's bedroom has a fancy Italian marble floor and windows that overlook the Pacific Ocean and downtown Los Angeles. Kobe's neighbors include actors Arnold Schwarzenegger and Tom Cruise.

Kobe wasn't the only new member of the Lakers. Mighty 7-foot center Shaquille O'Neal joined the team after four All-Star seasons with the Orlando Magic. The other Lakers looked to Shaq to lead them and quickly named him team captain. Shaq immediately nicknamed Kobe "Showboat." O'Neal said, "He shows a lot of poise for a high school guy. I can tell hanging around Kobe that he was raised very well."

**Kobe learned from his friend and teammate Eddie Jones.**

But was Kobe ready for the NBA? Lakers coach Del Harris had his doubts. Harris had been a pro coach for more than 30 years and once coached Jelly Bean Bryant. "Here's this kid in a man's game," Coach Harris said of Kobe. "He's not ready."

In Kobe's second game as a pro, a preseason practice game at the Forum against the 76ers, he received a loud ovation from the fans, topped only by the cheers for O'Neal. He flipped neat passes to teammates and made trick moves that embarrassed the Sixers, as the fans chanted "Ko-be! Ko-be!" In the third quarter, he stole a pass and whizzed down-court. Instead of taking the ball straight to the basket, he slowed down to wait for the nearest defender and then slammed the ball through at the last instant.

The 76ers thought Kobe was taunting them. The next time he got the ball, he went up for another slam, but Kobe was the one who got slammed. The Philadelphia center knocked him clear off the court. Kobe hit the floor hard and missed the rest of the preseason with a hip injury.

Kobe's foolishness bothered his teammates. "We have to watch his back," said O'Neal, "but I'm not here to be his father." Kobe's pal Eddie Jones said, "I told him after the game, 'The more you embarrass big guys by dunking the ball, the more they come after you and foul you hard.'" Guard Nick Van Exel also warned Kobe. "I told him not to showboat and embarrass people," he said.

Did Kobe get the message? Reporters asked Kobe the next day if he learned anything from the night before. Kobe sighed and then spoke as if he had re-hearsed the line "To prolong my career," he said, "I can't always attack the basket."

*As a rookie, Kobe was the youngest player in the NBA.*

# Learning
# on the Run

Fans filled the Forum on a balmy November night to see Kobe, who was barely 18 years old, become the youngest player in history to appear in a regular-season NBA game. With 2 minutes and 47 seconds left in the second quarter, Kobe stepped onto the court against the Minnesota Timberwolves. He played six minutes of the game, missed one shot, and made one rebound and one block. Kobe and his family, who were seated a dozen rows up from a corner of the court, were thrilled. "It'll be neat one day," Kobe said after the Lakers won the game, "to sit with my grandkids and tell them I was the youngest player in NBA history."

*Kobe's determination drove him to work extra hard.*

Kobe did not play more than a few minutes a game for the first month. Still, he impressed his teammates at practice. "I've never seen somebody who can see a move that another guy does and learn it as quickly as he can," said veteran Robert Horry. The players were surprised to learn that Kobe had gotten a set of keys to a high school gym so he could work out on his own. They were shocked to find out that he lifted weights every morning, even on a game day! "When Kobe came onto the team," said general manager Jerry West, "we said, 'What are we going to have to do extra for this kid? How are we going to watch over him?' But we haven't had to do anything. He's mature beyond his years."

Most NBA teams make their rookies do small tasks for the veterans. Kobe carried other players' luggage on road trips and sang songs to them on bus rides. Kobe had fun with such antics, but he preferred to do his entertaining on the court. Over the weeks, his playing time increased.

After Kobe made several great moves against the Utah Jazz, Coach Jerry Sloan said, "He's as talented as anybody who has ever come into the league." Kobe scored 19 points against the San Antonio Spurs and a season-high 21 against the Sacramento

Kings, though he barely played half of each game. Lakers assistant coach Larry Drew said, "Who does Kobe remind me of? He reminds me of Michael Jordan. I don't know how you can get that good that young. It's not natural, but that's what we've got here." Teammate Horry was asked if Kobe was fitting in with the team. "Fitting in?" Horry said. "Pretty soon other players will have to fit around him! Kobe is going to be the best player ever!" *The best player ever?* Better than the great Jordan? "Yep," Horry said. "Kobe's got Michael's skills and Michael's will. But Kobe came into the league when he was 18, and he's going to be able to accomplish more."

But off the court, Kobe did not fit in well with his teammates. Usually he did not even try. Most of Kobe's teammates were older than he was and had different interests. On road trips, the other players went to nightclubs. Kobe stayed in his hotel room and ate. (Kobe's favorite meal is breakfast, so he orders eggs, potatoes, and pancakes day and night at hotels.) After practices or games in Los Angeles, his teammates went to parties. Kobe preferred going home and splashing around in the swimming pool with his sisters. His two favorite hobbies are playing video games and reading the dictionary.

**To relax, Kobe and his friends play video games.**

Sometimes Kobe would call his high school pal Anthony Bannister. "He calls me at, like, three in the morning," Anthony said, "and we do all-nighters, writing rhymes." When Kobe did go out, he usually went with his sisters and their friend, Lisa Leslie, who plays basketball in the WNBA. They would go to cafés and practice speaking Italian.

Kobe also tried to improve his game. He studied players on videotape. He played great moves in slow motion over and over so he could learn them. "I really try to borrow things from every player," he admitted. "Michael Jordan's post-up, Reggie Miller's step back, little pieces and bits of every player. I'll take it and add it to my game."

His work paid off. A regular Lakers starter was injured, and Coach Harris rewarded Kobe. On January 28, 1997, Kobe became the youngest player ever to start an NBA game. A week later, Kobe grabbed the spotlight at the All-Star weekend by scoring a record 31 points in the rookie game. That night, he returned to the court for the slam dunk contest and became the first Laker to win it. On his final dunk, he passed the ball between his legs and jammed it with a windmill right hand to the roar of the crowd.

In games after the All-Star break, Kobe continued to show flashes of brilliance. When his team played the Bulls, he guarded the great Jordan and blocked one of Jordan's shots. "The kid is real good," Jordan said after the game. "I see a lot of myself in him."

In the deciding game of the conference semifinals against Utah, with the Lakers trailing by two, Coach Harris left Kobe on the floor for the final minute.

*Kobe's exciting dunks thrilled the All-Star crowd.*

*Despite the double-team, Kobe slips to the basket.*

Coach Harris told Kobe to take the game-winning shot—twice. Both shots hit nothing. The Lakers' season ended with two **air balls.** "Oh well," Kobe said, "It happens at every level you go. Whether you're in the sixth or eighth grade, you're going to make some shots to win the ballgame and miss some shots to lose the ballgame. Mine just happened to be on national TV."

The Lakers did not blame their 18-year-old star. "It's going to be real scary when he's 24, 25, 26 years old," said Shaquille O'Neal. "It's going to be real scary." Kobe did what he could to make sure of that. After the loss at Utah, the Lakers' airplane landed in Los Angeles at 2 A.M. A few hours later, Kobe was shooting alone in a high school gym. "And knowing Kobe," said Jerry West, "you can be sure he went to the same spot on the court where he missed those shots in Utah and started shooting."

*Kobe is an excellent free-throw shooter.*

# 5

# A Shooting Star

Kobe prepared for his second professional season by running sprints, lifting weights, shooting three hours a day, and playing in pickup games. And he didn't go to the University of California at Los Angeles just to play hoops. He took a full load of classes at UCLA over the summer. Kobe believes in exercising his mental muscles, too.

The 1997—98 season began with Kobe on the bench. It ended with Kobe as a starter and a star. In the season opener, he scored 23 points to lead the Lakers to a 104—87 win over the Jazz. Two weeks later at Utah, he blocked Bryon Russell's three-point attempt with five seconds left and slammed home a windmill dunk to seal a 97–92 victory. "He's improved leaps and bounds," 76ers coach Larry Brown said. "A lot was expected of him and he's answered everybody's doubts."

Kobe's impact on games was amazing. He went into one game with 15 minutes left and scored 27 points! He played the second and fourth quarters of another game and scored a career-high 30. As the team flew to Chicago for a midseason game against the defending champion Bulls, team officials warned Kobe that reporters would ask him about becoming the next Jordan. "It won't bother me," he replied. "I expect to be that good." Jordan scored 36 points in the game, but Kobe responded with 33 in much less playing time. Kobe also took the opportunity to learn something. "When we were at halfcourt, he asked me about my post move," said Jordan. "There is no question this kid is going to be something special."

Kobe was wildly popular in Southern California. His number 8 jersey even outsold Shaquille O'Neal's number 34. His popularity spread across the country, too. The shoe named after Kobe was outselling shoes named after Penny Hardaway, Grant Hill, Allen Iverson, and every other star except Jordan. Fans voted for Kobe to start in the All-Star Game.

*Michael Jordan and Kobe battle for the ball.*

"It's definitely cool, the fans acknowledging the hard work I did in the offseason," he said. O'Neal was asked about all the attention Kobe was getting. "Attention is like money," O'Neal said. "There's enough to go around for everybody."

*Kobe's aggressive style delights fans and draws fouls.*

Coach Harris made Kobe a regular starter at guard in mid-February. "It kind of messed up my system of bringing him along slowly, I must say," the coach said. With Kobe a key part of the team's offense, opponents began to **double-** and even **triple-team** him. "Early in the season, if I got by one guy, I was free," he said. "Not anymore." Kobe struggled. He began to force shots, sometimes with three or four defenders on him. A few of his teammates became angry. "I think they question my shot selection," Kobe said. "They never really say it to me, but I can just tell."

Worse yet, Kobe noticed that O'Neal hardly spoke to him. Other players whispered that O'Neal was jealous of Kobe. "Kobe's instant stardom and the way the crowd took to him really hurt Shaq," said one player. "Shaquille was supposed to be the marquee player." Kobe got pep talks from coaches and other players and tried to stay positive. "This is the toughest stretch I've ever gone through," he admitted. "But the more I learn, the better I will get. As far as jealousy toward me goes, that's high school stuff. I don't care what anybody thinks. I just play basketball."

Kobe changed his game. When defenders came at him in waves, he fought off his instinct to try to juke past them. He learned to pass the ball to open teammates. But he didn't learn that soon enough for some impatient teammates. They seemed to forget that Kobe was still a teenager learning the game.

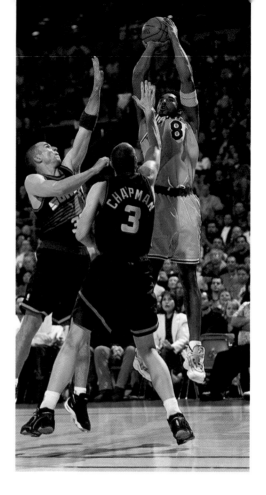

*Kobe always draws a crowd of defenders on the court.*

Kobe blamed himself. "I just had to learn to stop trying to do it all myself," he said. "You get caught up in a certain way of playing, and it's sometimes difficult to change your habits. And I was slow in doing that."

Kobe's **scoring average** (15.4 points) more than doubled from his rookie year. His **shooting percentage** actually went up, too. The expectations of Kobe were enormous, but no one's were higher than

Kobe's. "I want success," the young player said. "I'm going to spend the entire summer improving every aspect of my game."

Kobe worked hard on his passing and added 10 pounds of muscle with an intense weight-training program. The start of the 1998—99 season was delayed two months as the players and owners argued over salaries. Kobe took the extra time to work more on his game. The Lakers rewarded him with a new six-year contract for more than $70 million. When Kobe rejoined his teammates, he noticed some bitterness. In a preseason practice, Kobe and O'Neal exchanged words, and O'Neal slapped Kobe in the face. Punches were thrown before teammates broke up the scuffle. Magic Johnson, the team's vice president, tried to stop the feud. He told both players to be leaders and show that they could share the ball and the spotlight. Shaq scoffed at the idea. "They made me captain," he said, "so that's that."

Kobe started the season by holding Scottie Pippen to 1-of-10 shooting in the first half of a victory over the Houston Rockets. When O'Neal was asked about Kobe's suffocating defense, he replied, "Whoever was guarding Pippen was doing a good job." He would not even say Kobe's name.

*Shaquille O'Neal and Kobe have had to learn how to work together even though they aren't close friends.*

A few other players were also angry that young Kobe was becoming the team's star. "It hurts to see people want to see me fail," Kobe said, "but any time that has happened, I've just put it in my memory bank and said to myself, 'I'll show you.'"

Some suggested that Kobe should start spending time with his teammates off the court. Kobe wasn't interested. "I'm not out there trying to be Hollywood and club-hopping," he said. Kobe often felt lonely, especially on road trips, but he tried to make the best of it. In Orlando, for instance, when most of the players headed out to nightclubs, Kobe went to Disney World.

Coach Harris was fired midway through the year, and assistant Kurt Rambis replaced him. Despite the coaching change, Kobe's play did not suffer.

At Utah Kobe scored 24 points, as the Lakers snapped the Jazz's 20-game home winning streak.

*Kobe liked Coach Kurt Rambis, and the young star's game kept improving.*

Two weeks later, the Lakers trailed the Orlando Magic by 24 points, when Kobe took over. He scored 33 of his career-high 38 points in the second half to win. Kobe was shooting 46 percent from the field, the second-best percentage among shooting guards in the league. He was shooting better than Reggie Miller, Allan Houston, and Penny Hardaway. "If you really look at my numbers, they're pretty good," said Kobe. "I'm only 20 years old. This is only my third year in the league. I'm still improving. I'm trying to do the best job as I can. People want me to learn quickly, and that's what I'm trying to do. I'm trying."

Kobe's Lakers beat the Houston Rockets in the first round of the 1999 play-offs. But Tim Duncan and the San Antonio Spurs defeated Los Angeles in the semifinals. Throughout that season, Kobe learned some painful lessons about envy and acceptance. Forward Rick Fox was ashamed of his teammates. "We forget he's just a kid," said Fox. "We just sort of left him hanging this season, an island by himself, and that's going to stop. He wants to win as much as anyone else, and he deserves our support."

"My parents raised me to be an individual," says Kobe. "They taught me that there would be criticisms

*Sean Elliot guards Kobe during a 1999 play-off game.*

out there by many people, but you've just got to do what you think is right. The key to success at anything is to avoid peer pressure."

Kobe silenced his critics on and off the court with his performance in the 1999–00 season, which was capped by the Lakers' win of the 2000 championship series. Laker's coach Phil Jackson, who replaced Coach Rambis, was proud of what Kobe accomplished throughout the season and in the finals. "I think he's mature beyond his years . . . I think he has grown a lot in one year and yet I see a young man who's still got 13, 14 years of excellent basketball ahead of him," said Jackson.

Kobe's meteoric rise has made him a commercial success. He endorses everything from restaurants to the sodas served at them. Companies have put his name on shoes, basketballs, and so many video games that his friends call him Mr. Nintendo. Says one marketing pro, "For Kobe, the sky's the limit."

When Kobe isn't working on his game, he's helping around the house, taking out the trash or doing the laundry. "He comes home and it's just a normal life, nothing special," says his father. "I have the best of both worlds," Kobe explains. "Sometimes I feel like a kid, and sometimes I feel like an adult."

*Kobe missed the first 15 games of the 1999–00
season with a broken hand.*

Would he ever drink alcohol or try drugs? "No chance," he says. "My parents told me it wouldn't be good for my health."

Although Kobe may sometimes feel like a kid, he's a serious young man. In May of 2000, he announced his engagement to Vanessa Laine, whom he intends to mary before the 2000—01 season starts. But mostly Kobe is busy with a basketball. He has an inner drive that burns hot. "Kobe Bryant will be," Magic Johnson predicts, "one of the best clutch players in NBA history." Kobe is shooting for something even higher. "I want to be," he says, "the best player who ever set foot on a basketball court."

# Career Highlights

## Los Angeles Lakers

| Year | Games | Field Goals | | | Free Throws | | | Assists | | Points | |
| | | Made | Att* | % Made | Made | Att* | % Made | Total | Per Game | Total | Per Game |
|---|---|---|---|---|---|---|---|---|---|---|---|
| 1996–97 | 71 | 176 | 422 | 41.7 | 136 | 166 | 81.9 | 91 | 1.3 | 539 | 7.6 |
| 1997–98 | 79 | 391 | 913 | 42.8 | 363 | 457 | 79.4 | 199 | 2.5 | 1,220 | 15.4 |
| 1998–99 | 50 | 362 | 779 | 46.5 | 245 | 292 | 83.9 | 190 | 3.8 | 996 | 19.9 |
| 1999–00 | 66 | 554 | 1,183 | 46.8 | 331 | 403 | 82.1 | 323 | 4.9 | 1,485 | 22.5 |
| Totals | 266 | 1,483 | 3,297 | 45.0 | 1,075 | 1,318 | 81.6 | 803 | 3.0 | 4,240 | 15.9 |

*Attempted

- Set southern Pennsylvania high school scoring record, 1993–96
- Named National High School Player of the Year, 1996
- Became youngest player to appear in an NBA game, 1996
- Set All-Star Rookie Game scoring record with 31 points, 1997
- Won NBA Slam Dunk contest, 1997
- Became youngest player to start an NBA game, 1997
- Became youngest player to start in NBA All-Star Game, 1998
- NBA championship team, 2000

# Glossary

**air balls:** Shots that are missed in which the ball does not touch the backboard or rim.

**alley-oop:** A long, high pass to a player moving toward the basket that results in a dunk.

**backcourt:** The two guards who bring the ball up the court are called a team's backcourt.

**double-team:** When two defenders are guarding a player, he or she is facing a double-team.

**finger-roll layup:** A shot in which the player's hand is underneath the ball so that the ball rolls off his or her fingertips.

**goaltended:** A defender is not allowed to touch the ball when it is on its way down to the basket. If a player does touch the ball under these circumstances, he or she has goaltended it, and the basket counts.

**helicopter dunk:** A dunk that is preceded by the dunker moving his arms like a helicopter's blades.

**pickup games:** Informal games that are played between players who divide into teams, rather than between set, organized teams.

**scoring average:** The total number of points a player has scored divided by the number of games that player has played in. For example, let's say Kobe has played in five games and scored 25, 20, 15, 20, and 15 points in those games. If you add his point totals, you get 95. Divide that by 5 and his scoring average is 19.

**shooting percentage:** The number of shots a player makes divided by the total number of shots he or she takes. For example, let's say Kobe has taken 20 shots and has made 15 of them. If you divide 15 by 20, you get 0.750. Multiply the result by 100 to convert it to a percentage. In this example, Kobe's shooting percentage is 75 percent.

**triple-team:** When three defenders are guarding a player, he or she is facing a triple-team.

# Sources

Information for this book was obtained from the following sources: Michael Bamberger (*Sports Illustrated*, 6 May 1996); Ira Berkow (*The New York Times*, 27 February 1996); Clifton Brown (*The New York Times*, 27 June 1996); Ric Bucher (*The Washington Post*, 2 March 1998); Josh Chetwynd (*U.S. News & World Report*, 13 May 1996); Mark Emmons (*The Orange County Register*, 8 May 1999); Howie Evans (*New York Amsterdam News*, 5 February 1998); Ronald Grover (*Business Week*, 16 March 1998); Jaime C. Harris (*New York Amsterdam News*, 12 February 1998); Mark Heisler (*The Los Angeles Times*, 6 February 1998); Pat Jordan (*The New York Times Magazine*, 19 January 1997); Jeff Jensen (*Advertising Age*, 16 March 1998); Ben Kaplan (*Sports Illustrated for Kids*, May 99); Tim Kawakami (*The Los Angeles Times*, 9 May 1999); Jackie MacMullan (*Sports Illustrated*, 16 February 1998); Tom McEachin (*The Standard-Examiner*, 28 March 1998); Chris Mundy (*Rolling Stone*, 11 June 1998); Jim Murray (*The Los Angeles Times*, 15 February 1998); Bill Plaschke (*The Los Angeles Times*, 23 April 1999, 7 February 1999); Selena Roberts (*The New York Times*, 9 February 1998); Allison Samuels and Mark Starr (*Newsweek*, 16 March 1998, 31 May 1999,); Michael Sokolove (*Inquirer Magazine*, 1 March 1998); Lyle Spencer (*The Press-Enterprise*, 12 April 1998); Staff (*Harper's Bazaar*, April 1997); Phil Taylor (*Sports Illustrated*, 9 March 1998); Ian Thomsen (*Sports Illustrated*, 27 April 1998); Alex Tresniowski and Luchina Fisher (*People*, 31 March 1997); Michael Ventre (*Hoop Magazine*, May 1998).

# Index

## Write to Kobe

You can send mail to Kobe at the address on the right. If you write a letter, don't get your hopes up too high. Kobe and other athletes get lots of letters every day, and they aren't always able to answer them all.

Kobe Bryant
c/o Tellum and Associates
11911 San Vicente Boulevard
 Suite 325
Los Angeles, CA 90049

## Acknowledgments

Photographs reproduced with permission of: © Icon SMI, 1, 36, 44, 52, 57; SportsChrome USA, Michael Zito, 2, 48, 53, 58; © AFP/Corbis, 6; © ALLSPORT USA/Brian Bahr, 9, 13, 41; © ALLSPORT USA/Donald Miralle, 15; Classmates.com Yearbook Archives, 16; © Michael Freeman/CORBIS, 19; © ALLSPORT USA/Stephen Dunn, 25; © Lisa Rose/Globe Photos, Inc., 26; © Bruce Cotler/Globe Photos, Inc., 29; © ALLSPORT USA/Aubrey Washington, 32, 50; © ALLSPORT USA/David Taylor, 34; © Neal Preston/CORBIS, 39; © ALLSPORT USA/Andy Hayt, 42; © ALLSPORT USA/Jed Jacobsohn, 47; © ALLSPORT USA/Vincent Laforet, 55.

Front cover photograph by © ALLSPORT USA/Tom Hauck. Back cover photograph by © Fitzroy Barrett/Globe Photos, Inc.

Artwork by Tim Seeley.

## About the Author

Jeff Savage is the author of more than 80 sports books, including LernerSports biographies of Sammy Sosa, Jeff Gordon, and Julie Foudy. He and his family live in Napa, California.